MIRACLES

A Journey with Jesus — from His Life to Yours

JEFF LITTLE

www.milestonechurch.com
ISBN: 978-1-954961-14-2

Printed in the United States.

CONTENTS

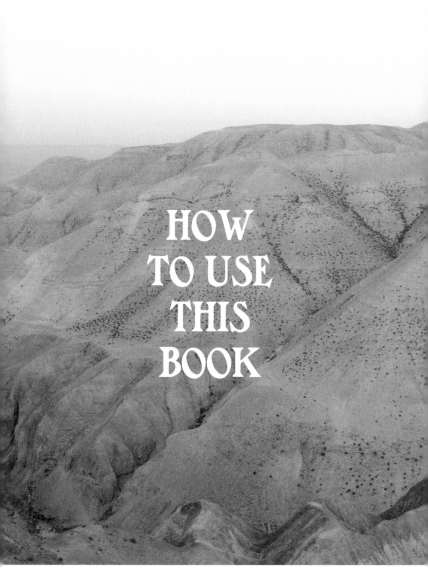

HOW TO USE THIS BOOK

Jericho Mountains

WATCH THE VIDEOS

To access the on-location videos
from Israel, scan the QR code at the
beginning of each chapter.

READ THE CHAPTERS AND
INTERACT WITH THE CONCEPTS

Underline key thoughts, write in the margins,
look up passages in your Bible, and answer the
questions at the end of the chapter.

TALK ABOUT
IT WITH A GROUP

To enhance your journey,
a Small Group Study Guide is included
in the appendix (p. 129).

Region of Tiberias

Preface

*"Miracles are not meant to be understood,
they are meant to be believed."*

D. Martyn Lloyd-Jones

Scan this QR code to watch my video from
the Region of Tiberias.

According to Merriam-Webster, a miracle is an "extraordinary event manifesting divine intervention in human affairs."

The Bible is filled with these moments.

This is one of God's most recognizable character traits—often, when they least expect it, He supernaturally intervenes in the lives of real people.

- He gives a barren couple (Abraham and Sarah) their first child when they are about 100 years old.[1]
- He gives the king of Egypt ten successive

---
[1] Genesis 21:1-7

miracles to deliver His people from slavery.[2]

- He parts the Red Sea for Moses and the people of Israel to walk through and escape the armies of Egypt.[3]
- He rains down bread from heaven to feed His people.[4]
- He levels the walls of Jericho after the people march and shout.[5]
- He refills the oil jar of a widow who thinks she's preparing her last meal.[6]
- He rescues a drowning man named Jonah by sending a giant fish to swallow him. Three days later, the fish spits Jonah back on the land.[7]

We cannot understand God or His Word without coming to terms with miraculous events we often struggle to explain or understand. For some, these insights create genuine intrigue and curiosity. For others, the mysterious details strain believability, making trust and faith more difficult.

One approach is to suggest these stories are merely fables, myths, or legends—spiritually themed moral tales not to be taken seriously.

For example, certain scholars counter that the Red Sea was more accurately referred to as "the sea of reeds," closer to a swamp than an ocean. Of course, this fails to

---

[2] Exodus 7–11
[3] Exodus 14
[4] Exodus 16
[5] Joshua 6
[6] 1 Kings 17:7-24
[7] Jonah 1–2

explain how the most powerful army in the world drowned in ankle-deep water.

Another common approach is to reserve judgment while suggesting that if we could see one for ourselves, we would be convinced. But the truly honest among us would admit we see things every day that we lack the ability to explain.

The Bible remains steadfast. Miracles are a feature, not a bug. They are a fundamental expression of both the nature and character of God.

The psalmist said, "You are the God who performs miracles; you display your power among the peoples."[8]

Neither magic trick nor metaphor, the story of God's relationship with human affairs consistently features His miraculous power in unique and surprising ways.

Consider a few more examples:

- Axe heads float.[9]
- The sun stands still in the sky.[10]
- Three young men survive a furnace so hot it kills the person tending it.[11]
- Man-eating lions lose their appetite.[12]
- A giant hand appears out of nowhere to write a message on the wall of a palace.[13]

---

[8] Psalm 77:14
[9] 2 Kings 6:1-7
[10] Joshua 10:1-15
[11] Daniel 3
[12] Daniel 6
[13] Daniel 5

You may be wondering, *What does this have to do with me? Does God still do these kinds of miracles? If so, how could I tell?*

And if He does, what kind of people experience this kind of supernatural intervention?

I'm honored you would take the time to pick up this little book on this very big subject. When it comes to miracles, I think most of us are in one of three groups. I'm sure there are more, but these cover the majority of our audience.

The first group in our professional, educated world struggles with how to make sense of miracles. Naturally, their instinct is to be skeptical. Fish that swallow people and seas that part with a dry path are not rational. They don't make sense. They sound like fairy tales.

This can be especially difficult for logical thinkers—or people whose worldview is deeply rooted in the scientific method. I appreciate the challenges this presents, and I am certainly not suggesting you have to turn off your critical thinking in order to engage in the discussion.

Often the question becomes, "Do I have to believe in this to have a relationship with God?" Or perhaps, "Can I trust a God who really wants me to believe this when I don't understand?" I get it. It makes sense to start from a posture of skepticism: "Prove it to me." The problem is, we all benefit from things we don't understand and see every single day.

Do you really understand how a combustion engine works? Can you see WiFi? Because we benefit every day from driving our car and being online, we don't spend a lot of time trying to understand exactly how it works.

Maybe you're more technical than me and clearly understand both of those processes. Let's think about this. Few things are more central to the human experience than love and pain. Can you prove love and pain? Can you see them? Does the absence of this somehow make them less real?

I realize in a few lines I am unlikely to convince you, but hopefully I have cracked the door just enough to get you to consider the possibility.

The second group is not sure but they're intrigued. They're curious. I have found most people *want* to believe in miracles; they see the value in wonder, awe, and mystery. They know life is better because of the presence of things we cannot explain.

Two of the most common questions with this group are "Why do some people receive miracles while others don't? Why doesn't God do it for everyone?" There is so much pain and suffering in the world. The temptation is to blame someone or to find a foolproof reason why sometimes it happens and sometimes it doesn't.

This is a big theological issue known as "theodicy." How can God be both all-powerful and good while evil and suffering still exist in the world? This issue is complicated. Far more intelligent people than me have debated it. We could spend the entire book discussing it.

My favorite response comes from Alan Plantiga, who argued that because God is good and wants to love and be loved by human beings, He gave us free will to prevent us from being coerced or acting like robots. With this, we also gained the ability to make choices that damage ourselves and others, resulting in widespread suffering and evil.[14]

Preaching the truth about who God is and how He's called us to live is so important. But like everything in a relationship with God, in the end it comes down to *trust* more than spiritual principles and propositional truths.

Do we believe God is good? Do we believe He loves every person and has a plan to redeem and restore them? If we are confident in both of those, does it really matter how and when He chooses to do it?

We can trust Him. And His Word is true. Both of them work together. Hebrews 2:4 says God confirms preaching through miracles, signs, and wonders.

---

[14] This is my best attempt to summarize his classic, "Free Will Defense," from 1974's *God, Freedom, and Evil.*

Finally, the third group believes in, and prays for, miracles. Most of them would say they have experienced God's miracle power and expect to again at some point in the future. When Jesus made His triumphal entry into Jerusalem, Luke 19 says the people praised Him for the miracles they had seen. Perhaps the most common response to God's miracle power in our lives is to worship Him.

While most people would like to receive a miracle, very few of us want to be in a place where we need one! But one of the most encouraging aspects of the miracle stories in the Bible is the fact they are not restricted to the elite, the powerful, or the self-righteous. In most cases, God sent miracles to the people who felt overlooked, forgotten, unimportant, or on the margins of life.

I have been asked many times throughout the years, "Is there something I am supposed to do to make a miracle happen?" This is a challenging question—especially because many of the miracles are connected to health and healing. This can cause people to feel condemned because they feel they don't have enough faith or don't know the exact words to pray.

A simple answer like "If you prayed more or if you believed God more passionately . . ." does not give the total picture. We do not manipulate God into doing something He does not intend to do.

And yet, at the same time, the Bible does connect our faith, our trust, and our willingness to believe Him with experiencing His miracle power. During several miracles (we will look at a couple later), Jesus tells the person receiving the miracle, "Your faith has made you well."

As a loving Father, God never gets upset when His children ask Him for help. It also does not mean His answer is always yes or that He answers us in the way we expect.

But He does want us to ask. He is near to the brokenhearted.[15] He does not distance Himself from people who need a miracle—their heartfelt cries catch His attention and move Him to meet them in the middle of their crisis.

My goal with this little book is to help you get closer to Jesus. Along the way your understanding of the Bible will grow. You will have greater insights into the customs and context of Jesus' culture, which will help you apply what you learn to your daily life.

This book is not a 6-step process to ensure you will receive a miracle anytime you need one. My intention is not to put that kind of pressure on you. But this doesn't make the goal less important.

---

[15] Psalm 34:18

There is no denying the Bible is filled with miracles. Miracles show us the nature and character of God. And the same God who divinely intervened in the lives of real people is present and active in your life.

I am not promising how or when God will intervene in your life. But as we go on this journey together, I know He is going to reveal Himself to you in a powerful way.

He promises when we draw near to Him, He draws near to us.[16]

Whether you are struggling to make sense of miracles, you are intrigued, or you are praying and believing for one, I want all of us to be clear on why we are going through this study together.

Miracles do not prove the existence of God. He is God whether or not we acknowledge Him.

But the miracles of Jesus demonstrate the power of God working in and through Him. They change the way people relate to Him. While He did use them to punctuate His teaching, they also substantiated He was from God in the eyes of the people.

When Peter preached the first message after the resurrection on the day of Pentecost, he reminded them Jesus was accredited by God through the miracles, the signs and wonders, God did for them through Jesus.[17]

---

[16] James 4:8
[17] Acts 2:22

He is more than a wise teacher speaking about conceptual spiritual principles.

Jesus is the Son of God who moved in miracle power as He conquered sin, death, and the grave.

Is, not *was*.

And this Jesus wants to be close to you. He wants you to know Him. More than anything else, miracles are an invitation to know and worship Jesus, and to see Him for who He truly is.

I can promise you, anyone who invests their time and energy to know more about the God who still performs miracles will grow closer to Him.

Let's begin this journey together with an open heart and a clear sense of expectation.

The Southern Steps of the Temple Mount

Introduction

*"Jesus's miracles are not a challenge to
our minds, but a promise to our hearts, that
the world we all want is coming."*

Timothy Keller

Scan this QR code to watch my video
from the Southern Steps.

The more things change, the more things stay the same.

This is difficult to remember because the way we do life is
constantly impacted by the accelerated rate of technolog-
ical advances.

There was a time when the TV broadcast went off late at
night. There were only a few channels, and eventually they
would play the National Anthem and the screen would turn
to static "snow."

Not that long ago you couldn't talk to someone on the phone unless it was plugged into the wall. Parents did not know where their kids were or what they were doing. Somehow we survived.

It was not normal to carry a supercomputer around in our pockets, so we interacted with strangers if we were waiting in line, we looked at the road while we were driving, and we talked with people as we shared a meal.

Our kids (not to mention our grandkids) will never understand that world.

But as much as things have changed, human nature remains the same. We still have the same needs. We want to give and receive love. We want to be known. We wrestle with our identity and our purpose.

Which ultimately means we want to know God.

This is why we relate to the characters in the Bible. Although they lived in a completely different culture, at the deepest level we share the same struggles.

The details are different but the problems, and our instinctive reactions to them, are the same.

We both feel distant from God. We both wonder how He feels about us. When we face challenging circumstances, we both assume He either doesn't know or He doesn't care.

This explains why miracles are so important.

A miracle is a touchpoint where heaven breaks into earth. It is a supernatural demonstration that God is not distant, He is not unaware, but He is near and He cares for our needs.

And no one regularly demonstrated this more than Jesus.

This was bigger than miracles—it was also what He preached. He was more than a guy with a few tricks, like Pharaoh's magicians or Simon the Sorcerer.[1] When He performed miracles, like healing the sick, multiplying food, and casting out evil spirits, it was consistent with what He taught and how He lived.

This was not what He did; this was who He was.

Everything Jesus did and said was an expression of His character as the Son of God.

He did things only God could do. He claimed He had the power to forgive sin.[2] He said anyone who had seen Him had seen the Father.[3] He referred to Himself using God's holiest name.[4] And He received worship—from the time of His birth to some of His most memorable moments.[5]

---

[1] Exodus 7:11, Acts 8
[2] Matthew 9:6
[3] John 14:9-10
[4] John 8:58
[5] Matthew 2:2, 11

When He walked on the Sea of Galilee and rescued Peter, they didn't say, "Wow...that was cool!" Everyone who was in the boat bowed down and worshiped Him. They said, "Truly you are the Son of God."[6]

Jesus is the exact representation of the Father. Fully God and fully man. Messiah, Savior, and the King who comes to announce the arrival of God's Kingdom—life as God always intended it to be.

We feel far from God because He is "other," which is what the word "holy" means.[7] He is uncreated, perfect, and without need. We struggle to relate to Him.

It's true we have been created in His image, but the impact of sin has corrupted the design like a virus. Our mirror cracked. Our reflection is broken.

In His goodness and mercy, God takes it upon Himself to solve this crisis. Instead of a bureaucrat, an official, or even a servant, He sends His only Son to us.

Jesus comes near to us. He is the living expression of the love of God. He does not stay in the perfection and security of eternity and heaven.

He comes close.

---

[6] Matthew 14:33

[7] The word "holy" (Hebrew *kadosh*) literally means to be separate, apart, or sacred. It communicates the idea that God is separate from everything else in life. He is completely "other."

Across the four Gospels, there are approximately 40 times when Jesus performs a miracle. Because John ends his Gospel explaining that he did not tell every story of all the incredible things Jesus did, we know there were more.[8]

While it may not seem like a big deal, this detail is significant. If miracles were the goal, John would spend less time on Jesus and more time chasing down these stories. Instead, he prioritizes and emphasizes the person of Jesus.

John spends nearly half his Gospel on the events surrounding Jesus' betrayal, arrest, crucifixion, and resurrection, ensuring the reader understands what truly matters.

We find the story of Jesus' first miracle in John 2. Jesus and His friends and family are at a wedding in Cana. In the ancient world, wedding celebrations would often last up to seven days. The celebration was more like an open house than a scheduled ceremony, which made planning and preparing for the event difficult.

Jesus' mom tells Him the guests have run out of wine. She doesn't tell Him because she knows He likes to party. She tells Him because she loves this family and she knows run-

---
[8] John 21:25

23

ning out of wine at a wedding is a major social *faux pas* that could make this family the village joke for years to come.

Initially, Jesus is reluctant because He knows a miracle like this will accelerate His timeline. He is right. John tells us this was the first sign that revealed Jesus' glory and His disciples believed in Him.

Jesus is balancing His compassion for people with His Father's larger purpose. Those two things are not at odds with each other. His Father's larger purpose is always an expression of His love and mercy.

The tension comes down to the timing and details. This was true for them and it continues to be true for us.

Like them, we often interpret apparent silence from heaven as punishment or a lack of love. When we don't get the answer we want on the timetable we need, we assume this is a sign of God's displeasure.

This is a flaw in our fallen nature—we know this because our relationship with God is not the only place where it shows up.

If your boss mentions, "We need to have an important conversation," most of us do not think, *Great news!* Our first thought is closer to, *Uh-oh. What did I do wrong?*

This can make us suspicious and nervous. We may try to avoid them. We certainly don't feel close to them. While this creates tension in our workplace, the consequences are much greater when it comes to our relationship with God.

Too many people see God this way. They think He's indifferent, uncaring, or even looking for a reason to punish them.

Remember, because miracles demonstrate the character and nature of God, no matter what need they have, the primary message Jesus wants them to receive is how much God loves them.

So how does Jesus want us to think about miracles?

Jesus was very clear on the unhealthy expectations regarding miracles.

For example, two of the villages near where He grew up had a hard time making sense of what was happening. Because Jesus was from there, because they knew His family, they were skeptical. They did not believe God was working through Him.

Jesus told them that if the miracles He performed there had taken place in some of the most notorious pagan cities in the region, they would have turned their hearts toward God and believed.[9]

Not much later, some religious leaders came to Him demanding a sign. Jesus refused. He told them wicked and unfaithful people demand a sign. He told them the only

---

[9] Matthew 11:20-24

sign they would receive would be when He was placed in a tomb for three days before being resurrected.

They thought He was getting His power from the forces of darkness and so they wanted to evaluate Him. He told them that one day people in history who repented without seeing what they had seen would stand and convict them for their unbelief.[10]

Essentially, Jesus is saying our posture toward miracles should not be skepticism or pride. It never ends well for us. We have no right to demand God's miracle power or to sit in judgment of it.

Instead, we should trust that God loves us and believe at any time He can intervene on our behalf. When, if, or how that happens does not change how good He is or how much we can trust Him.

Throughout all of Scripture, and especially Jesus' ministry, miracles were participatory. The first part is always divine compassion. God is moved by the cries of Egypt, so He miraculously sets them free.[11]

---

[10] Matthew 12:38-42
[11] Exodus 3:7-10

When Jesus sees a family on the edge of embarrassment, He supernaturally turns water into wine. As we will see, this was only the beginning of a wide variety of signs and wonders.

We won't look at all 40, or try to uncover the ones beyond that, because it only takes one to see His heart for people.

While miracles always start with God's love for people, the second part often involves faith from the person who trusts God enough to ask.

We will see this pattern repeated over and over.

It's not self-help. It's not a secret formula, a hidden process, or something God owes us. Faith always trusts in a person. It is a deep expectation of the goodness of God.

Miracles aren't contracts or transactions. God is never obligated to us. Miracles are relational. Because they grow out of trust, they strengthen our connection to God and result in wonder and praise.

As we turn to look at six specific miracle stories, we need to remember that Jesus never got upset at anyone for believing God too much. He never condemned anyone who asked for a miracle with a good heart.

Instead, He saved His strongest correction for the skeptical, the arrogant, and the unbelieving.

This is not easy for us. We prefer to hedge. We want to guard ourselves from the pain of unmet expectations.

My goal for you is to grow closer to God as you learn and experience more of His heart. I want you to stay away from unhealthy imbalances.

God is a miraculous God, but the signs are not an end to themselves. They point us to Him.

We are encouraged to have faith and trust God, but I am not saying the reason you haven't received the miracle you're praying for is because you don't have enough faith.

I want to invite you to go on this journey with me with an open mind and a willing heart. The best example of what this practically looks like comes from a miracle story I mentioned in the Preface.

Three young men are threatened with death by an angry king because they won't bow down and worship him. He threatens them with death by a fiery furnace and asks what god will be able to save them.

They respond by saying, "The God we serve is able to save us from you and your furnace, but even if He doesn't, we're not bowing down and worshiping you."[12]

I love their hearts. What a great example for how God wants us to relate to Him. We believe God can do anything, but whatever He does, we are still going to trust and love Him.

I don't think you can ever go wrong with this approach.

---

[12] This scene is from Daniel 3:13-18.

The Sea of Galilee

ONE

WHAT HAPPENS IN THE STORMS OF LIFE?

Scan this QR code to watch my video from the Sea of Galilee.

Fear is part of the human condition.

None of us are immune to the effects of fear.

While snakes, spiders, sharks, clowns, and zombies terrify a lot of people, very few of us regularly come in contact with them. Without much effort, we can avoid them.

The real dangers are the things we encounter every day.

- Kids are afraid of the dark.
- Teenagers are afraid of missing out.
- Moms and dads fear for the health and future of their children.

- Leaders can be afraid of failure and success—at the same time.
- Early in your career, you worry about opportunities.
- Later in life, you worry about your legacy.
- People of all ages are afraid of ending up alone.

All these fears are legitimate. Life is hard. No one escapes the storms of life. And there is no shortage of things to be afraid of.

We have access to more information than ever before and so we have more reasons to be afraid. And when everyone is fighting for our attention, fear becomes one of the most effective ways to grab us.

Not only are we afraid of the things we know about, but we're also constantly worried about the things we don't know. Fear of the unknown is one of our most common maladies.

The ocean makes people afraid. Think about this: Although more than 70 percent of the earth is covered by the ocean, more than 80 percent of this area remains unexplored.[1]

We don't know what's out there. It makes us feel small and sends our imagination running to the scariest possible outcomes.

---

[1] https://oceanservice.noaa.gov/facts/exploration.html

Because there are many ways to die on the ocean, these fears are not irrational. People were afraid of it in the ancient world—some are afraid of it still today.

I realized this personally several years ago when I was on the Sea of Galilee. Our team was preparing to shoot videos and work on a message on a boat that would take us across the lake. We grabbed our things and made our way onto the boat, got settled, and headed out to open water.

At some point we realized one of our team members wasn't there. We couldn't find him—until we looked back at the shore. He was briskly walking up the ramp leading away from the water after deciding he wasn't ready for the voyage.

We all face fear. The question is, what do we do when we're afraid?

Some of us run. Some of us try to fight through it. Some of us close our eyes and hope it goes away.

And some of us pray for a miracle.

The Sea of Galilee looking toward Mount Arbel

The Sea of Galilee is also referred to as Lake Gennesaret or Lake Tiberias. Because it does not immediately connect to the ocean, it is a large lake (64 square miles, 157 feet at its greatest depth) that often behaves like a sea.[2]

Much of Jesus' earthly ministry occurred in this region around this body of water. One story, recorded in three of the four Gospel accounts, happened after a long period of Jesus teaching large crowds. He told the disciples to get in the boat in order to cross the sea. They were not excited about this news. Across was the wrong direction.

This was not a relaxing evening cruise after a long day's work. Jesus had an intentional plan and He only included those who were committed.

Matthew's version of the story includes the detail of teachers and other boats wanting to accompany Jesus and His disciples, but He challenges their commitment and so they disappear from the story.[3]

Luke's version is preceded by Jesus' mother and brothers asking for Him to come and He responds that His mother and brothers were those who put what He taught into practice.[4]

[2] https://www.britannica.com/place/Sea-of-Galilee
[3] Matthew 8:18-22
[4] Luke 8:19-21

Jesus was teaching His followers what it means to trust God in challenging circumstances. He's still teaching that message today.

Most fishermen in Capernaum stayed close to the shore because the winds and the unique conditions on the lake made deeper waters more dangerous, and small fishing boats were not prepared for squalls. Warm temperatures cause constant evaporation in large bodies of water (especially in this part of the world) and the lake is surrounded by steep hills, which causes the hot, wet air to circulate.

The combination of the Mediterranean climate with the lake's location 696 feet below sea level led to violent downdrafts triggering sudden sea storms.

Mark includes the detail of Jesus sleeping on a cushion in the stern of the boat, which demonstrates both His fatigue from ministry life and His total lack of concern for His own safety.

The disciples, and the people hearing the story later, would have likely connected what happens next to the story of Jonah. Jonah ran away from God's call because he didn't care for the people he was called to reach.[5] Jesus kept moving toward the people because He loved them, even though He knew many would not receive Him.

---

[5] Jonah 1

MARK 4:35-41, ESV

[35] On that day, when evening had come, he said to them, "Let us go across to the other side." [36] And leaving the crowd, they took him with them in the boat, just as he was. And other boats were with him. [37] And a great windstorm arose, and the waves were breaking into the boat, so that the boat was already filling. [38] But he was in the stern, asleep on the cushion. And they woke him and said to him, "Teacher, do you not care that we are perishing?" [39] And he awoke and rebuked the wind and said to the sea, "Peace! Be still!" And the wind ceased, and there was a great calm. [40] He said to them, "Why are you so afraid? [41] Have you still no faith?" And they were filled with great fear and said to one another, "Who then is this, that even the wind and the sea obey him?" [6]

This was more than some choppy water and a little sea-sickness. The disciples were afraid and genuinely worried about their lives because this was certainly a dangerous situation.

---

[6] Highlighting key phrases or words while we're reading Scripture can help us focus and get more out of our reading.

The passage implies they believed they were going to ship-wreck and drown. They were so worked up that they were more hurt and offended than afraid because they couldn't believe Jesus was unwilling to do anything to help.

Jesus was disappointed because they were so afraid and they failed to believe He could save them.

The pagans believed great heroes, angels, and the gods could control the weather, but the Jews believed God alone controlled the weather and the oceans.[7] The disciples were not expecting this.

With only three simple words, Jesus miraculously calmed the storm and saved their lives.

Their perception of who He was and what He could do was forever changed.

---

[7] Psalm 18:15

All of the disciples understood the potential for a dangerous storm to pop up on this kind of trip. They were keenly aware of the risks and the numerous ways this journey could go horribly wrong.

But none of them expected Jesus to be the One to save them.

We are a lot like them in so many ways.

Every day we are confronted with information and opinions warning us of life-threatening challenges and potential danger. In the midst of these conditions, God calls us to obey and follow Him.

This leaves us with a choice: do we shrink back in fear or move forward in faith?

When we recognize the reality of storms, danger, and serious adversity, how often do we respond the same way they did? It's more than fear.

We fall for the lie that the presence of these challenges somehow means God neither sees us nor cares if we die.

Meanwhile, He has never done anything to substantiate this feeling. In fact, the opposite is true. He's with us, in perfect peace, and is in total control of our situation.

The real storm isn't in the waves; it's in our hearts.

We have a hard time trusting He's really good and that He will save us. We can get so consumed by our miracle need that we lose sight of the One who has miracle power.

Our greatest hope in God is not that He's more powerful than us; it's in the fact that He is more loving, more faithful, and His goodness is more than we can possibly imagine.

Even when it does not make sense.

Remember, the miracles never point to themselves. They always point to the nature and character of God.

Peace is not dependent on the wind and the waves. It is not dependent on our circumstances.

True peace, the kind that can overcome fear, pain, and every form of suffering, comes from God.

It is always available to those who put their trust in Him.

The Dead Sea

REFLECTION QUESTIONS

What is a storm you are facing in your life right now?

After reading this chapter, what did you learn about Jesus?

You can ask Jesus to help you in your storm.

Personalize this sample prayer and make it your own.

> *Jesus, I believe you see me in my storm and you care about what I'm facing. Please help me in my need* [describe your situation here]. *You asked us to have faith, so I put my trust in you. You said in Luke 11:9-10 to ask, seek, and knock in prayer, because the one who asks will receive. Thank you for hearing me. I believe you're working in this situation for my good. In Jesus' name I pray. Amen.*

Roads outside of Jerusalem

TWO

FROM THE OUTSIDE IN

Scan this QR code to watch my video from a road outside of Jerusalem.

We've all experienced the pain of rejection.

- "You're not good enough."
- "You'll never amount to anything."
- "No one likes you."
- "No one wants you around."

The effects of these words can leave a mark lasting years and even decades. Being shunned by those we admire leaves us wounded. Maybe you were picked last on the playground at recess. Maybe you stood alone on the edge of the dance floor.

No one wants to live on the outside stuck in the margins of life. Most of us don't know what to do about it.

45

As our world has become increasingly polarized and isolated, many are demanding universal inclusion while threatening to cancel the noncompliant. This is not how relationships work. This is not how healthy societies work.

Genuine and meaningful connection is offered, not institutionalized.

Jesus understands this, and unlike us, He has the ability to bridge the gap.

He demonstrates this throughout Scripture. He was always looking to the margins because He came to seek and to save the lost. He went to those who society, culture, and especially religious leaders discarded, and offered them a place in His Kingdom if they would repent and receive the Good News.

In the ancient world, groups were marginalized on the basis of age, gender, ethnicity, heritage, religion, politics, occupation, and physical health. This type of prejudice was common.

Another prevailing belief was that people became sick as punishment from the gods. Good people enjoyed good health. Bad people were struck down.

The sick were routinely quarantined or abandoned and left to fend for themselves, especially if the disease was contagious. Child mortality rates were so high that a common estimate was that every other child died before they could enter adolescence or adulthood.

One of the ways people insulated themselves from this level of incredible emotional pain was to devalue or minimize their emotional connection with their children.

Jesus intentionally broke down these barriers. Children. Women—and women caught in adultery. Roman soldiers. Samaritans. Tax collectors. The blind. The demonized. Lepers.

He loved them, healed them, and received them into His Kingdom when they repented and received Him. This is an important detail.

Jesus always meets us where we are, but He never leaves us there.

While He affirms our value as children created in the image of God, He calls us to change our thinking, the affections of our heart, and the patterns of our lifestyle.

Old olive tree looking toward Bethlehem

Luke, a physician and a ministry companion of the apostle Paul, is the only Gospel writer who includes this amazing story.

The road between Galilee and Jerusalem went past Samaria. Many of the Jews would avoid it because of their strong dislike for the Samaritans. The Samaritans were descendants of a group of Israelites who separated to follow other religious practices. They became a haven for malcontent, rebellious, or deconstructing Jews. However, there were cultural Samaritans who remained faithful in their affection and commitment to the God of Israel.

Hebrew men would make the pilgrimage to Jerusalem at least three times per year to celebrate festivals. There were three primary paths they could take. The direct path past Samaria took only three days.

The second path went east over the Jordan River, and then back over the Jordan again around Jericho on the way to Jerusalem. It took five to seven days and passed villages like Bethpage and Bethany, where Mary, Martha, and Lazarus lived.

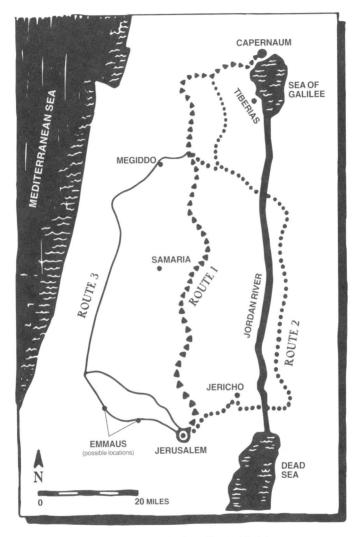

Jesus intentionally chose Route 1 to take
His disciples by Samaria on their way to Jerusalem.

The third path went west by the Mediterranean Sea and was the longest route as it passed Megiddo and Emmaus.

Jesus chose to take His disciples along the route that went through Samaria,[1] even though it was culturally taboo. As they passed this region, they came upon a village. Outside the village they interacted with a group of ten men with leprosy who stood at a distance from them as a courtesy.

These ten men would not have been allowed into the village because the contagious nature of their disease would have endangered the other people in the village. Remember, the prevailing belief was that their disease was a sign of God's judgment.

"Leprosy" was a catch-all term for any infectious skin disease. It did not always refer to the technical condition. Any infectious skin disease put you in quarantine and made you a social castaway. Because of this, the term "leper" refers as much to social outcasts as the actual degenerative skin disease.

Once you were labeled a leper, it eclipsed all your other social distinctions. It became your identity. Samaritans had low social class, but a Samaritan with leprosy was simply a leper.

---

[1] Jesus did it again when He encountered the Samaritan woman at the well in John 4. It also explains why the parable of the Good Samaritan would have been shocking to His audience.

LUKE 17:11-18

¹¹ Now on his way to Jerusalem, Jesus traveled along the border between Samaria and Galilee. ¹² As he was going into a village, ten men who had leprosy met him. They stood at a distance ¹³ and called out in a loud voice, "Jesus, Master, have pity on us!" ¹⁴ When he saw them, he said, "Go, show yourselves to the priests." And as they went, they were cleansed. ¹⁵ One of them, when he saw he was healed, came back, praising God in a loud voice. ¹⁶ He threw himself at Jesus' feet and thanked him—and he was a Samaritan. ¹⁷ Jesus asked, "Were not all ten cleansed? Where are the other nine? ¹⁸ Has no one returned to give praise to God except this foreigner?"

When Jesus sent the lepers to show themselves to the priest, in their minds they had to believe He was setting them up for rejection. This was a terrible idea. Priests observed strict guidelines to remain ritualistically clean. They were not allowed to share any space with a leper. There was no way for a leper to go see the priests.

But Jesus told them to do it anyway. And when they obeyed Jesus instead of their feelings, they were healed.

This is worth considering. Have you thought about how our willingness to step outside of our comforts or expectations impacts our ability to receive from God? There is a pattern to these miracle stories with Jesus.

Often, the one who is willing receives more than the one who appears spiritual or has the greatest need.

These ten were not healed instantly; they were only healed "as they went."

There was another outsider God healed of leprosy. Naaman was a great commander of the army of the king of Aram. He had leprosy and his wife (from Israel) told him to go see the prophet Elisha. Elisha told him to wash seven times in the Jordan River. Naaman got mad; he wanted Elisha to simply pray and heal him. But one of Naaman's servants convinced him to do it, and after the seventh time, his skin was made brand new.[2]

Same God. Same miracle. A different approach but it required the same participation: faith and obedience.

Imagine what this healing meant to these ten lepers. It was so much more than eliminating a potentially fatal disease. It also removed the stigma. It was redemptive in every possible way. They could return to their families. Potentially they could get married and have children.

They were free to pursue the life God created them to live.

---

[2] You can find this story in 2 Kings 5:1-15.

It was more than healing—it was a whole new life.

This healing reveals God's heart for people shunned and left on the outside. Those on the margins. Those who have been rejected.

The love of God is so redemptive that it never stops simply at addressing our immediate needs.

It doesn't just restore us to the village; it brings us into God's family. Jesus had more than pity on them; He had purpose.

He invited them to join Him in His Kingdom. It is an invitation to eternal life. This eternal life is more than life that never ends. It speaks to more than quantity—life everlasting. True eternal life is about quality of life, the Greek word *zoe*. It is the perfect life we were created by God to experience and enjoy.

When Jesus prayed in the Garden of Gethsemane on the night He was arrested, He said, "Now this is eternal life: that they know you, the only true God, and Jesus Christ, whom you have sent."[3]

This is the gospel message for all of us, no matter what our presenting need. It's more than a ticket to heaven—as

---

[3] John 17:3

wonderful as that will be. It begins today. We can experience it now.

This is why it is always a miracle when we are adopted into His Kingdom. We are born again. New creation breaks into the old world of our hearts.

Miracles do more than reveal the character of God; they also show us who we are. Unfortunately, once we receive what we've asked for, we tend to lose some of our passion and desperation.

Our hunger for God has a way of shrinking back to our level of need.

Ten lepers were healed by Jesus. Ten lives forever changed. Ten outsiders immediately restored. Ten captives set free. Ten supernatural fresh starts. Ten miracles.

But only one returned to Jesus to thank Him. He threw himself at Jesus' feet in the most humble and public demonstration he could offer. And this one was a Samaritan. He was the one most likely to feel undeserving, on the outside, without connection to this Jewish Messiah.

Despite his cultural distance, he saw something the others did not. Somehow he understood that what he had received was bigger than new skin and the opportunity to pursue a full life. Heaven had broken through to earth. Through Jesus, God had come near.

What about the other nine? What was more important than being closer to Jesus? The story doesn't tell us, but they weren't the only ones who got distracted.

When God gives you a miracle, when He answers an incredibly important prayer, how do you respond? The temptation is to feel relief, to relax, or to simply move on.

Most of us don't like to ask for help. It makes us feel small and vulnerable. We would much rather admit we have it all together—even when we don't.

Too many times, when God answers our prayer and helps us, we act like we had it under control ourselves. Especially when we are more interested in solving our problems than growing in our relationship with God.

If we're honest, as long as we're alive we will continue to be dependent on God. Like these nine men, most people are only as desperate for God as their needs require.

But who says we have to live that way? We can be like this Samaritan, this outsider, who figured out one of life's most valuable lessons.

Who God is, is better than what He does.

We were created to be close to Him. Jesus said that the best way to understand eternal life, the life we were created to live, is knowing God.

This is the greatest miracle. And Jesus offers it to all of us. We can receive this miracle new every morning.

REFLECTION QUESTIONS

When was the last time you hesitated to step outside of your comfort zone because you were uncertain of the outcome? Can this keep you from receiving from God?

After reading this chapter, what did you learn about Jesus?

When you feel stuck, held back, or left on the outside, you can call on Jesus.
Personalize this sample prayer and make it your own.

> *Thank you, Jesus, for not playing it safe. Thank you for taking the direct route to my life. I know you came looking for me before I ever searched for you. When I'm uncertain and hesitate to trust you—whether in my relationships, my health, my finances, my work situation* [pick your biggest issue now]*—give me the courage and faith to step out. I know many times we receive our miracle as we're going. In Jesus' name I pray. Amen.*

Ruins of the Great Synagogue of Capernaum

THREE

WAITING ON A MIRACLE

Scan this QR code to watch my video from the ruins of the synagogue of Capernaum.

A miracle always starts with a need or a problem. This means if you have a need or a problem, you're an ideal candidate for a miracle.

It doesn't matter where we live, how old we are, how successful we've been, or who we know—we all have problems and needs.

Everyone wants a miracle—no one wants to need one.

And one of the hardest parts is the waiting.

We live in an on-demand world. Everything is instant. Press a button on your phone and it's on its way.

Amazon trucks spend more time in our neighborhoods than the mailman and the ice cream truck combined. It's not just pizza anymore. DoorDash will bring us whatever we want to eat.

You can't DoorDash a miracle.

It's the waiting that gets us. No one likes to wait. It's easy to believe technology can save us from having to wait. Waiting is old-school. We think waiting is wasted time.

But some of the most important things in life only come through waiting. And some things are worth the wait.

Something powerful happens when God's people come together and pray. Jesus said in Matthew 18:19, when two people agree in prayer about anything, they can ask the Father and He will do it for them.

Lots of churches have times of dedicated prayer. Our church starts the year with a concentrated time of prayer and fasting we call "Prepare." One of the things we do is invite people to write their prayer requests on cards and post them on a wall so others can pray and agree with them.

Every time I walk through and read them, I'm moved by the genuine needs of the people. It gives me a small picture of what God feels for His people and their faithful prayers.

I am always struck by how some people have been waiting for years for their miracle, like the salvation of a family member or the restoration of a relationship.

Others don't have that option. Their window is much smaller. Their prayer is for a financial miracle or the health of a loved one and they need an answer within days or even hours.

Whether the deadline is 24 hours or open-ended, waiting for a response can tempt us to question the character of God. Is He still good? Does He see? Does He care?

Will we continue to trust and believe in His goodness and faithfulness when the answer does not come? When the sand is running out in the hourglass? When the clock is about to strike midnight and the end is coming fast?

As long as there have been people, we have wrestled with this challenge. The Bible says this is how it works. We receive the promises of God through faith—trusting in His goodness—and patience, the willingness to wait.[1]

We trust God to do His part while we recognize we have a part to play. His part is to deliver on the promise of His Word.

---

[1] Hebrews 6:12

Our part is to ask for His help, even when we're uncertain and afraid, when we feel unworthy or unqualified, or when we're disappointed because it feels like it's not working while we're waiting.

Remember, the waiting is never meant to be wasted.

More than giving us His promises, God cares about who we become in the waiting.

He wants to develop our trust in Him, build our character, grow our faith, and transform us into the kind of people who can comfort and encourage others in their time of need.

When Jesus calmed the Sea of Galilee and crossed to the other side, He ministered to people on the other side. But when He and the disciples went back, they found a large crowd of people waiting for Him. They had heard about His teaching and how when He prayed for the sick, God healed them. They wanted to see for themselves.

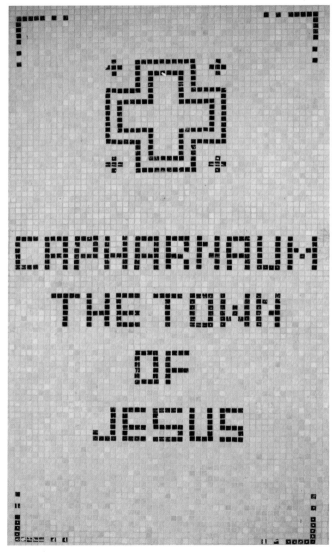

Mural leading into the ruins of Capernaum

Jesus ran into two people with miracle needs. One was a man, the other was a woman.

The man was a city leader named Jairus whose only daughter was sick and dying. He fought through the crowd to get to Jesus, threw himself at Jesus' feet (not a common move for important people), and begged Him to come pray for His only child.

His need was immediate.

The woman had been struggling for 12 years with bleeding. This caused her to be viewed as unclean. This was not arbitrary; it was clearly addressed in the Bible.[2] The purpose behind this was not meant to be shameful, embarrassing, or mean, but it did cause her to live her whole life as an outsider.

In the ancient world, they did not have a drugstore on the corner to get all their basic hygiene products. They could not afford to transmit germs or blood through casual contact without endangering the food and water supply of the community.

The social contract had to be upheld for the common good. Ignoring these standards was not a cool way to express yourself; it put the lives of people you cared about in danger.

Her need had lasted 12 years.

---

[2] Leviticus 15:25-30

On the one hand, their situations were very different. The woman had been waiting for years, while Jairus could not wait another moment.

And yet in so many ways their needs were the same.

Jairus's daughter was 12 years old. She was on the verge of moving from a child to a young woman. Her entire life covered the same span the woman had been struggling with her bleeding.

Both of them had placed all their hopes on Jesus. He was here. Close enough to talk with. Close enough to touch. If God was going to heal them, this was the time.

LUKE 8:40-56

40 Now when Jesus returned, a crowd welcomed him, for they were all expecting him. 41 Then a man named Jairus, a synagogue leader, came and fell at Jesus' feet, pleading with him to come to his house 42 because his only daughter, a girl of about twelve, was dying.

As Jesus was on his way, the crowds almost

crushed him. ⁴³ And a woman was there who had been subject to bleeding for twelve years, but no one could heal her. ⁴⁴ She came up behind him and touched the edge of his cloak, and immediately her bleeding stopped.

⁴⁵ "Who touched me?" Jesus asked.

When they all denied it, Peter said, "Master, the people are crowding and pressing against you."

⁴⁶ But Jesus said, "Someone touched me; I know that power has gone out from me."

⁴⁷ Then the woman, seeing that she could not go unnoticed, came trembling and fell at his feet. In the presence of all the people, she told why she had touched him and how she had been instantly healed. ⁴⁸ Then he said to her, "Daughter, your faith has healed you. Go in peace."

⁴⁹ While Jesus was still speaking, someone came from the house of Jairus, the synagogue leader. "Your daughter is dead," he said. "Don't bother the teacher anymore."

⁵⁰ Hearing this, Jesus said to Jairus, "Don't be afraid; just believe, and she will be healed."

⁵¹ When he arrived at the house of Jairus, he did not let anyone go in with him except Peter, John and James, and the child's father and mother. ⁵² Meanwhile, all the people were wailing and mourning for her. "Stop wailing," Jesus said. "She is not dead but asleep."

⁵³ They laughed at him, knowing that she was

dead. **54** But he took her by the hand and said, "My child, get up!" **55** Her spirit returned, and at once she stood up. Then Jesus told them to give her something to eat. **56** Her parents were astonished, but he ordered them not to tell anyone what had happened.

Healing often happened through prayer and the laying on of hands. In Mark's account of this story, Jairus specifically asked Jesus to come and lay His hands on her because he knew it was important.

But both of these situations were complicated in this regard. You can't touch the sick or the dead without becoming unclean.

Matthew's and Mark's versions explain that the woman thought that if she could just touch Jesus' clothes, she would be healed. This was a thoughtful act of consideration. She knew according to Scripture that if she touched Jesus, she would make Him unclean, so as a courtesy, she put all her faith into touching His clothes.

Mark tells us she had spent everything she had on doctors in hopes she would be healed, but instead of getting better, she got worse. But when she touched Jesus, she was immediately healed.

Jesus knew the moment it happened, but He wanted the disciples, the crowd, and especially the woman to understand.

The disciples were clueless. Jesus asked them who touched Him, and Peter basically said, "It's a crowd! Everyone is touching you."

Because everyone's eyes were on Jesus, and He stopped to investigate, the woman knew she'd been discovered. She was nervous and afraid. She was expecting to once more be treated like an outsider, an unclean annoyance. But in her gratitude, she explained her plan and how it had worked.

Instead of correcting her, Jesus celebrated her faith. He lovingly affirmed her. He intentionally used loving, familial language. He did more than heal her. He changed her identity.

He called her "daughter." She left with more than her healing. She left with a whole new understanding of God as her loving Father.

You have to wonder how Jairus was handling this interruption by an unclean woman. His daughter's life was on the line and this woman delayed them.

It would have been so easy for him to blame her. He was the one who got to Jesus and convinced Him to come.

And at that moment, his worst fear came true. The news came from his house that it was too late. His daughter had died. Jesus understood how hard this was for Jairus. He told him not to be afraid but to believe.

Notice that when they got to the house the people were wailing and mourning. Jesus told them to stop. That's a bold move. They were so emotional that they laughed at Him and mocked Him because they knew she was dead. Jesus sent everyone out except for His closest disciples and Jairus and his wife.

Jesus told them the girl was not dead; she was asleep. Then He did the very thing Jairus initially asked for—He took her by the hand. Jairus would never have asked for this because touching a dead person would have made Jesus unclean.

Jesus took her by the hand. God came close enough to touch. Her spirit returned to her, just like when Elijah prayed for the widow's boy in 1 Kings 17:22.

But Jesus was not Elijah. Something greater was happening here. Everyone who saw what happened was astonished, but Jesus ordered them not to say anything because it was not time for everyone to know He had the power to raise the dead. That would come later.

Jairus and the woman believed God had the power to heal. But they did more than believe; they took steps by faith. They participated. They asked boldly, but they were also willing to wait, trusting in the nature and character of God.

And like He always does, God gave them more than their healing. He gave them a new picture of His goodness and character. He changed the way they related to Him.

He brought them close. Even when it looked like their hope was gone and everything was getting worse, the waiting was not wasted.

He wants to do the same for us.

We need to remember this the next time we find ourselves with a miracle need. Yes, Jesus sees and cares. He invites us to bring all of our burdens to Him.

Whether we wait years, hours, or minutes, He has a purpose and a plan.

It probably won't happen the way we expect.

But His promise is bigger than meeting our needs. He wants to build our faith. He wants to come close enough to touch. He wants to change the way we see Him.

The waiting does not have to be wasted.

REFLECTION QUESTIONS

What is a need you've been waiting for God to meet? How long have you been waiting? Have you given up or are you still trusting Him to meet you?

After reading this chapter, what did you learn about Jesus?

Jesus will meet you while you're waiting for your miracle. *Personalize this sample prayer and make it your own.*

> *Jesus, you said it's through faith and patience we inherit the promises of God. I trust you are working in the waiting. Jesus, I'm asking you to remember my need* [fill in your specific need]. *No matter how long I wait, I will put my trust in you because I believe I will see your goodness and your faithfulness as I continue to believe your Word. In Jesus' name I pray. Amen.*

Village ruins at Capernaum

FOUR

MIRACLES WITH FRIENDS

Scan this QR code to watch my video from the ruins of a village at Capernaum.

Human beings were created for connection and friendship. We don't do well on our own.

But friendship requires commitment, sacrifice, and generosity. Friendship changes our perspective from "me" to "we."

Over the past several decades, our culture has continued to become increasingly individualistic, prioritizing personal preference and self-expression. We are told, above all else, to be true to ourselves.

According to this narrative, genuine happiness is found by looking inward and expecting the outside world to adapt to our needs.

The results have been devastating.

We live in the era of "virtual connection." Technology, the internet, and social media make us feel like we are surrounded by everyone and known by no one.

On May 3, 2023, the Surgeon General issued an advisory on our "epidemic of loneliness and isolation." Research shows you can be lonely with people constantly around you because loneliness is about the *quality* of your connections.

This is bigger than an emotional issue. It carries very real physical dangers. This lack of relational connection leads to a 29 percent increased risk of heart disease, a 32 percent increased risk of stroke, a 50 percent increased risk of developing dementia, and a 60 percent increased risk of premature death.[1]

I have worked with people long enough to realize that life brings plenty of trouble to each of us. It does not matter how successful we are, how much money we accumulate, and how comfortable our lifestyles become.

We are either in a storm, coming out of a storm, or headed for a storm someday down the road. When the storm comes, it is too late to find friends to help.

---

[1] Office of the Assistant Secretary for Health (OASH), May 3, 2023. *New Surgeon General Advisory Raises Alarm About the Devastating Impact of the Epidemic of Loneliness and Isolation in the United States.* HHS.gov. https://www.hhs.gov/about/news/2023/05/03/new-surgeon-general-advisory-raises-alarm-about-devastating-impact-epidemic-loneliness-isolation-united-states.html.

The friendships we make today prepare us for the storms of tomorrow.

Proverbs 17:17 tells us that a friend loves at all times. Every one of us would love to have this kind of friend. This begs the question, where do you find that kind of friend? The simple answer is to first *be* that kind of friend for someone else.

This kind of friendship is not a coincidence or a luxury. It is a life-saver. We can't survive without it.

Once you've experienced this kind of genuine friendship, you understand how rare and incredibly valuable it is. It is a gift from God.

And it can even open the door for miracles.

The crowds surrounding Jesus had become so large that people could not get close to Him.

Do you remember the last time you were in this kind of crowd?

Synagogue ruins in Capernaum

Maybe you were at a sporting event or a concert at a large stadium. It can be disorienting. All of the commotion and activity demand concentration, but at least there are tickets and ushers to help you reach your intended destination.

The ancient world was not so convenient.

The people were excited because Jesus was healing the sick and teaching with genuine authority. While the crowds continued to grow, He would withdraw to lonely places to pray,[2] only to reappear later with miracle power.

Some were curious to see what this was all about.

The religious leaders were skeptical and critical.

And then there were those who were in desperate need of help from God. They would do whatever it took to get close to Him.

This story is about a group of friends in a desperate situation. We don't know how many there were. We don't know how they knew each other. We don't know their names or where they came from.

We don't know how far or how long they traveled to be close to Jesus.

All we know is that their friend was paralyzed and confined to a mat, and they loved him so much that they carried him through the crowd.

---

[2] Matthew 14:23

LUKE 5:17-26

¹⁷ One day Jesus was teaching, and Pharisees and teachers of the law were sitting there. They had come from every village of Galilee and from Judea and Jerusalem. And the power of the Lord was with Jesus to heal the sick. ¹⁸ Some men came carrying a paralyzed man on a mat and tried to take him into the house to lay him before Jesus. ¹⁹ When they could not find a way to do this because of the crowd, they went up on the roof and lowered him on his mat through the tiles into the middle of the crowd, right in front of Jesus.

²⁰ When Jesus saw their faith, he said, "Friend, your sins are forgiven."

²¹ The Pharisees and the teachers of the law began thinking to themselves, "Who is this fellow who speaks blasphemy? Who can forgive sins but God alone?"

²² Jesus knew what they were thinking and asked, "Why are you thinking these things in your hearts? ²³ Which is easier: to say, 'Your sins are forgiven,' or to say, 'Get up and walk'? ²⁴ But I want you to know that the Son of Man has authority on earth to forgive sins." So he said to the paralyzed

81

man, "I tell you, get up, take your mat and go home." **25** Immediately he stood up in front of them, took what he had been lying on and went home praising God. **26** Everyone was amazed and gave praise to God. They were filled with awe and said, "We have seen remarkable things today."

A friend would offer to take you to Jesus. A good friend would actually fight through the crowds as they carried you through. But only a great friend would not give up when they finally discovered there was no room and no way to get close to Jesus.

Most houses did not have stairs inside, but roof access was possible along the stairs on the outside of the building. Refusing to be denied, these friends dragged him to the roof and then had the boldness to interrupt whatever Jesus was doing inside by lowering their friend down to Him.

Instead of being angry or annoyed, Jesus was moved by the courage and faith of these friends. Before they even had a chance to explain, Jesus called this paralyzed man "friend" and forgave his sins.

Miracles do more than meet needs—they reveal the nature and character of God.

Jesus knew that everyone in the crowd was watching closely. He could have prayed for him to be healed. But He wanted to reveal something about who He was and what He came to do.

That was the first time He confronted the religious leaders in public. He would do this many more times over the next few years, not only for their sake but to change the perspective of the people watching.

He was more than a prophet who spoke for God. He was more than a man with a gift of healing. He said He had the power and the authority to forgive sin. Only God could forgive sin.

Once a year, on the day of atonement, the high priest would go and offer sacrifices in the temple on behalf of the people. The reason the religious leaders called Jesus a blasphemer was because they rightly understood the significance of what He was doing.

Jesus was effectively saying He had come to replace that system.

To many of us, it sounds like Jesus changed the subject, but on that day all the people understood. The prevailing belief was that people who were paralyzed (or had any other form of serious illness) were in that condition because of someone's sin—either their own, their parents, or some other ancestor in their family line.

Therefore, to forgive the sin was to deal with the root cause of the illness. Jesus knew this would create an uproar. He wanted to force that reaction because He wanted the people to wrestle with who He truly was.

He is more than a cosmic healer passing out miracles and making dreams come true. Jesus is a King who invites sinners to be born again and enter His Kingdom.

Because Jesus is Lord, He refuses to be a means to someone else's end. He will not go quietly into someone else's box. He will not be less than who He truly is.

He wouldn't do it then. He won't do it now.

Everyone wants to see a miracle; no one wants to need one.

And perhaps the only thing more challenging than needing one yourself is to need one for someone you love whom you feel powerless to help.

A church is more than powerful music and inspiring messages. Jesus called the Church His body. We are meant to carry one another's burdens. Jesus told us when we gather together in His name, He's with us. When we agree and pray in His name, we can ask Him anything.

This is why we ask for prayer requests. It's why we take time in the middle of our worship services to read and pray over specific needs. This is how a family cares for each other. Something powerful happens when God's people come together and pray for one another.

I'm reminded of this every time someone comes up and tells me, "You prayed for my request last week…and God answered my prayer!" If it happened one time to me it would be enough but it routinely happens to our team. Every week our staff and pastors pray over every single request that comes in because this is what churches do.

This is part of what it means to be a spiritual family. Which brings me back to where we started.

None of us are meant to carry our needs on our own.

God promised to build His Church because it's His hands and feet, His body on the earth, to accomplish His purpose and to bring His presence.

We don't know these friends' names, how far they had traveled, or what happened to them after this moment, but

Jesus responded to them. Their friend picked up his mat and walked home, praising God the whole way. Everyone else was amazed too.

Do you have friends who love you enough to bring you to Jesus in your storm? Or perhaps more importantly, do you have people you love so much you'd be the one to carry them?

You might be thinking, *Jeff, what does that mean? I don't even know where to start?* I get it. But it's simpler than you think. You don't have to know everything about the Bible or have all the answers to their questions.

Like these friends, you can bring your friends to Jesus. For example, you could invite them to come to church with you to help them grow in their relationship with God. It's amazing how often people come when they're intentionally asked.

You could also show up in their need. I am consistently moved by the generosity and love of the people in our spiritual family. When I show up at the hospital or at a difficult situation, I'm rarely the first one on the scene. They're anticipating and meeting practical needs and demonstrating the love of Jesus however they can.

When you receive this kind of love, you never forget it.

Jesus wants all of us to live with these kinds of connections.

Not only can He meet our needs, but He can heal our souls.

Where else in life can we find this? In ourselves? Self-help books have never been more popular, because we love the idea that we can fix ourselves.

But we didn't stop with self-help. Now we have "self-care" and "self-love." But no matter how much we love telling ourselves this story, there's a problem. It does not work.

And as great as they are, the ultimate goal is not friendship or connection. Those are wonderful gifts, but sooner or later a storm comes that's too big for our friends. In those moments, the friend we need is the one who knows how to get us to Jesus.

REFLECTION QUESTIONS

Do you feel like you have the kinds of relationships who would take you to Jesus in your moment of need? If not, are you connected to a church family?

Who are you praying for with this kind of need? Write their names below. What can you do to practically show them the love of Jesus?

After reading this chapter, what did you learn about Jesus?

Jesus loves it when we pray and believe for our friends.

Personalize this sample prayer and make it your own.

> *Jesus, help me to be the kind of friend who loves and serves others. I want to love people the way you love them and connect them to you. Help my friend* _____ [put your friend's situation here]. *Give me the courage to step out when I'm afraid, the patience to overcome obstacles, and the wisdom to know what to do. In Jesus' name I pray. Amen.*

The Mount of Olives overlooking Bethany

FIVE

FINDING JESUS IN OUR DEEPEST PAIN

Scan this QR code to watch my video from the Mount of Olives overlooking Bethany.

One of our natural defenses against worry and anxiety is to project our fears and concerns to their ultimate outcomes. Most of us do this to prepare ourselves, strengthen our resolve, and get our emotions ready for what might happen.

We ask ourselves this question: What's the worst that could happen?

Psychologists call the constant and unnecessary use of this defense "catastrophizing" and view it as detrimental to our long-term health.[1] Our bodies react to this heightened emotional state as if this worst-case scenario is actually happening.

---

[1] https://www.psychologytoday.com/us/basics/catastrophizing

The problem comes from the repeated false alarms and dress rehearsals that weaken our ability to face genuine crises. Not only do we risk losing trust from our support system and earning the reputation of being a little dramatic, but it also impacts our emotional health.

Repeatedly turning relatively minor emotional 2s into 10s prevents us from the stability required to face an actual 10.[2]

Which leads us to the question, how will we respond to the worst-case scenario? No one is ever prepared to face life's deepest pain, but those moments have a way of finding us.

Even when it's not our fault. Even when it's no one's fault.

In this kind of desperation, we cry out to God for help. We need a miracle.

Does He see us?
Does He care?
Will He help?

There's an old saying in the military: There are no atheists in foxholes. When the danger is great enough to face our own mortality—or perhaps more emotionally, when our loved ones are staring death in the face—we cry out to God.

---

[2] Imagine a scale where a 1 is a minor inconvenience and a 10 is a life/death situation.

Several of Jesus' friends found themselves in this exact situation. The journey they went on over the next few days pushed them beyond their limits and stretched everything they believed about God.

Luke tells a story where Jesus and His disciples were traveling through a village and they were invited into a home by a woman named Martha.[3] Her sister, Mary, sat and listened to everything Jesus said while Martha kept busy working to provide everything their guests needed.

Martha got frustrated and asked Jesus to tell Mary to help, but Jesus insisted that Mary had made the better choice: to be close to Him.

John tells us that Mary and Martha had a brother named Lazarus, and Jesus loved him and called him His friend.[4] Lazarus became very sick, so the sisters sent word to Him. Jesus had recently been ministering close to where this family lived but things had gotten heated. He was so clear about His relationship with God and His own divinity that the religious leaders picked up stones to kill Him.

---

[3] Luke 10:38-42
[4] John 11:1-3, 5

The disciples were not excited to go back. They were afraid. But Jesus told them they were going so that God would be glorified, because Lazarus's sickness would not end in death.

Jesus waited a few days and then He told the disciples it was time to go. They tried to talk Him out of it, so He told them Lazarus had fallen asleep and He needed to go wake him up. The disciples tried one more time. They suggested that if Lazarus was sleeping, he would feel better eventually.

Finally Jesus ended the debate. He explained that Lazarus was dead. It was time to go. The fact that Jesus waited and did not go right away is an important part of the story. He was showing the disciples, this family, and everyone who hears this story something vital about God's character.

John makes sure we know how much Jesus loved Mary and Martha.[5] Just because He waited did not mean He did not love them. Something bigger was happening.

John also includes the detail that Thomas, who was no stranger to catastrophizing, sarcastically said, "Let's go so we can end up dead too!"

---

[5] John 11:5

JOHN 11:17-44

¹⁷ On his arrival, Jesus found that Lazarus had already been in the tomb for four days. ¹⁸ Now Bethany was less than two miles from Jerusalem, ¹⁹ and many Jews had come to Martha and Mary to comfort them in the loss of their brother. ²⁰ When Martha heard that Jesus was coming, she went out to meet him, but Mary stayed at home.

²¹ "Lord," Martha said to Jesus, "if you had been here, my brother would not have died. ²² But I know that even now God will give you whatever you ask."

²³ Jesus said to her, "Your brother will rise again."

²⁴ Martha answered, "I know he will rise again in the resurrection at the last day."

²⁵ Jesus said to her, "I am the resurrection and the life. The one who believes in me will live, even though they die; and whoever lives by believing in me will never die. Do you believe this?"

²⁷ "Yes, Lord," she replied, "I believe that you are the Messiah, the Son of God, who is to come into the world."

²⁸ After she had said this, she went back and called her sister Mary aside. "The Teacher is here," she

said, "and is asking for you." **29** When Mary heard this, she got up quickly and went to him. **30** Now Jesus had not yet entered the village, but was still at the place where Martha had met him. **31** When the Jews who had been with Mary in the house, comforting her, noticed how quickly she got up and went out, they followed her, supposing she was going to the tomb to mourn there.

32 When Mary reached the place where Jesus was and saw him, she fell at his feet and said, "Lord, if you had been here, my brother would not have died."

33 When Jesus saw her weeping, and the Jews who had come along with her also weeping, he was deeply moved in spirit and troubled. **34** "Where have you laid him?" he asked.

"Come and see, Lord," they replied.

35 Jesus wept.

36 Then the Jews said, "See how he loved him!"

37 But some of them said, "Could not he who opened the eyes of the blind man have kept this man from dying?"

38 Jesus, once more deeply moved, came to the tomb. It was a cave with a stone laid across the entrance. **39** "Take away the stone," he said.

"But, Lord," said Martha, the sister of the dead man, "by this time there is a bad odor, for he has been there four days."

40 Then Jesus said, "Did I not tell you that if you believe, you will see the glory of God?"

> ⁴¹ So they took away the stone. Then Jesus looked up and said, "Father, I thank you that you have heard me. ⁴² I knew that you always hear me, but I said this for the benefit of the people standing here, that they may believe that you sent me."
>
> ⁴³ When he had said this, Jesus called in a loud voice, "Lazarus, come out!" ⁴⁴ The dead man came out, his hands and feet wrapped with strips of linen, and a cloth around his face.
>
> Jesus said to them, "Take off the grave clothes and let him go."

Lazarus had been dead for four days. He was not sleeping. Jesus wanted to make sure there was no mistaking what was taking place.

Notice how both Martha and Mary had the same initial reaction. They both told Jesus that if He had been there, their brother would not have died. We don't know if this is because He made them feel safe or because Jesus was so well-known for healing the sick.

Their precise intention is not the main point. They are following the very human pattern of blaming God for their pain. We think the avoidance of pain means God loves us. John goes to great lengths to make sure we understand that is not the issue.

The fact that we face pain is not a sign God does not love us. The opposite is true. Pain, especially great pain, shows us how nothing can separate us from God's love.

The Garden Tomb

His love for us is bigger than the greatest pain we can go through: death itself.

Some people know "Jesus wept" is the shortest verse in the Bible, but most people don't know why He was crying. Jesus is (not was) a great friend.

Jesus' tears reinforce this so clearly. He knew in a moment that Lazarus was going to walk out of the tomb to be reunited with his family. Death was not going to win. But Jesus was so moved by the depth of their love that He wept. He did not sit back from a distance. He met them in their pain. He showed them they were not alone.

Aren't you grateful Jesus is so much more than a stoic religious leader or a historical figure captured by paintings and statues?

Jesus has not changed. Sometimes He waits. He always comes on His schedule. But He still meets those who love Him in their deepest pain. He always shows up. He is never absent. He does not look from a distance. He comes close to be with us, to comfort us, and to triumph over death.

Jesus performed roughly 40 miracles. None of them were like this one.

Raising Lazarus from the dead was the turning point of Jesus' ministry. The religious leaders accelerated their plans to kill Him. The people worshiped Him at the Triumphal Entry. Within a week He would be betrayed, arrested, beaten, crucified, and placed in a tomb.

All of this set the table for the ultimate miracle.

Like Lazarus, Jesus would rise from the dead. But unlike Lazarus, He would take on the sin of the world and offer His perfect, sinless life as a sacrifice for all of humanity.

In Jesus, the consequences of sin that separated a perfect God from sinful human beings were removed.

Death itself was defeated, and He would rise with a glorified, eternal body.

The resurrection remains the greatest and most meaningful miracle in all of human history.

We all carry the tendency to catastrophize. To protect ourselves, we think, *What's the worst that can happen?* And then based on our personality, we take that projection and run with it.

The problem is, we mix up the meaning.

Remember, miracles do more than meet our needs; they reveal the character of God.

The greatest part of this story is not the fact that Lazarus walked out of the tomb, alive and restored to his family. The real beauty is the way Martha, Mary, and Lazarus now saw God in a completely different way.

What's the worst that could happen? Death. Four days in the tomb. The body is rotten and smells.

Who can overcome this? God. Did He do it the way we expected? No. But we can be sure He sees us, He loves us, and He comes near.

REFLECTION QUESTIONS

Few things can make us feel distant from Jesus like pain. Are you carrying significant hurt and pain? Write it down. Have you invited Him into it?

After reading this chapter, what did you learn about Jesus?

Jesus may not come on our schedule, but He always meets us in our pain.

Personalize this sample prayer and make it your own.

> *Lord, I'm struggling with _____ [fill in your specific need]. I don't want to carry this anymore. I don't want it to dominate my life. I don't want to be tempted to blame it on you. Jesus, I believe you are a great friend who loves me and will meet me in my pain. I'm asking you to come with your resurrection power and heal my heart. In Jesus' name I pray. Amen.*

The Sea of Galilee

SIX

THE SECOND FIRE

Scan this QR code to watch my video from the shore of the Sea of Galilee.

Miracles are real.

Because God is good, He is present in our lives and He is in complete control. At times He supernaturally meets our needs with His miracle power.

And many times we don't even realize the miracle is happening until later. He's constantly moving and working in our lives, even when we don't see it. That's how good He is.

But why does God perform miracles? What's the point?

Over the course of the book, I have been making the case that the primary reason He does this is to show us who He is. His goal is to bring us closer in our relationship with Him through a deeper trust and understanding of His love for us.

Relationships are not meant to set up miracles. God needs no setup. If His goal was to show us His power, He could overwhelm us at any point.

Unfortunately, even when confronted with insurmountable evidence, some of us still would not believe.

Have you ever noticed the little phrase right before the Great Commission in Matthew 28? The disciples were with the resurrected Jesus; they could see Him as He literally ascended in the heavens.

"Some doubted."[1]

Think how crazy that is. These were not skeptics or religious critics. They were the disciples. And yet they still doubted.

It shows that no matter what God does, some people will still struggle to believe.

Miracles do not force us to believe, but they invite us into a greater connection to God.

---

[1] Matthew 28:17

They can bring us closer.

The purpose of miracles is to strengthen our relationship with God. This is why our participation is so important. It's also why Jesus would comment on the faith of the person trusting God to move.

Their faith, combined with God's goodness displayed through His miracle power, changed them.

When God does the impossible, not only does it change us, but it also changes the people around us. He's always doing more than we realize. He works in us to work through us.

Because miracles bring us closer and strengthen our relationship with God, they also remind us of everything God has done in the past.

We have short-term memories. Especially in crisis. We get trapped in the pressure, in our own emotions, and in the lies of the enemy. It can be shocking how easy it is to forget the incredible things God has done.

Imagine being one of Jesus' original disciples. The week leading up to His death and resurrection begins with the incredible celebration of Palm Sunday. Jerusalem, the great

LES OUTRAGES CHEZ CAIPHE

Site of the house of Caiaphas where Peter denied Jesus

Dungeon beneath the house of Caiaphas where Jesus was held the night before His crucifixion

city, is filled with people shouting in praise. You would feel so validated and excited.

There are ups and downs throughout the week until you come to Thursday.

You share the most meaningful and emotional Passover Supper ever with Jesus. He promises to go and prepare a place for you in eternity with His Father. He prepares you for coming challenges with the most insightful discussion of the Holy Spirit in human history.

He takes you to the garden to pray, and soon, soldiers come and arrest Him. They throw Him into the prison under the high priest's house. Very early the next morning He is put on trial and then beaten so brutally He's barely alive. Then He's mocked and paraded through the streets until He's hung on a cross outside of town.

You watch Him die. He mentioned it would happen, but you didn't really believe it. And then He's thrown in a tomb surrounded by soldiers so no one can steal His body and falsely claim He was resurrected.

Imagine the devastation you would feel. Was any of it real? What about all the things He had promised? What about the incredible miracles? Was all of it for nothing?

Now imagine you were Peter. You were the closest to Jesus. You were the one to walk on the water with Him for a moment.[2] You were the one who boldly declared He was the Messiah.[3] You were the one who grabbed a sword and foolishly tried to defend Him in the garden.[4]

And you were also the one who denied Him three times around a fire on the night He was betrayed—just as He said you would.[5]

What would you do? Probably the same thing most of us would do. You would go back to what you know. Jesus had already appeared to them several times, but they felt like such massive failures.

They were overcome with guilt and shame. They felt so unworthy. Jesus would have to find someone else more dependable and qualified. So what would you do?

You would return to the old job you left when He first called you.

For Peter, this was fishing. Peter and his brother Andrew were partners with James and John. We know this because Luke 5 tells the miraculous story of how Jesus first calls them to follow Him. Without this context, what happens in John 21 is interesting but not nearly as meaningful.

Jesus is doing much more than helping them catch fish. He restores a broken relationship. He heals wounded trust. He

---

[2] Matthew 14:22-33
[3] Mark 8:27-30
[4] John 18:10
[5] John 18:15-18, 25-27

helps a man who feels like a failure rediscover his purpose and calling.

And the whole world is different because He did.

JOHN 21:1-22

¹ Afterward Jesus appeared again to his disciples, by the Sea of Galilee. It happened this way: ² Simon Peter, Thomas (also known as Didymus), Nathanael from Cana in Galilee, the sons of Zebedee, and two other disciples were together. ³ "I'm going out to fish," Simon Peter told them, and they said, "We'll go with you." So they went out and got into the boat, but that night they caught nothing.

⁴ Early in the morning, Jesus stood on the shore, but the disciples did not realize that it was Jesus.

⁵ He called out to them, "Friends, haven't you any fish?"

"No," they answered.

⁶ He said, "Throw your net on the right side of the boat and you will find some." When they did, they were unable to haul the net in because of the large number of fish.

[7] Then the disciple whom Jesus loved said to Peter, "It is the Lord!" As soon as Simon Peter heard him say, "It is the Lord," he wrapped his outer garment around him (for he had taken it off) and jumped into the water. [8] The other disciples followed in the boat, towing the net full of fish, for they were not far from shore, about a hundred yards. [9] When they landed, they saw a fire of burning coals there with fish on it, and some bread.

[10] Jesus said to them, "Bring some of the fish you have just caught." [11] So Simon Peter climbed back into the boat and dragged the net ashore. It was full of large fish, 153, but even with so many the net was not torn. [12] Jesus said to them, "Come and have breakfast." None of the disciples dared ask him, "Who are you?" They knew it was the Lord. [13] Jesus came, took the bread and gave it to them, and did the same with the fish. [14] This was now the third time Jesus appeared to his disciples after he was raised from the dead.

[15] When they had finished eating, Jesus said to Simon Peter, "Simon son of John, do you love me more than these?"

"Yes, Lord," he said, "you know that I love you."

Jesus said, "Feed my lambs."

[16] Again Jesus said, "Simon son of John, do you love me?"

He answered, "Yes, Lord, you know that I love you."

Jesus said, "Take care of my sheep."

[17] The third time he said to him, "Simon son of

John, do you love me?"

Peter was hurt because Jesus asked him the third time, "Do you love me?" He said, "Lord, you know all things; you know that I love you."

Jesus said, "Feed my sheep. **18** Very truly I tell you, when you were younger you dressed yourself and went where you wanted; but when you are old you will stretch out your hands, and someone else will dress you and lead you where you do not want to go." **19** Jesus said this to indicate the kind of death by which Peter would glorify God. Then he said to him, "Follow me!"

20 Peter turned and saw that the disciple whom Jesus loved was following them. (This was the one who had leaned back against Jesus at the supper and had said, "Lord, who is going to betray you?") **21** When Peter saw him, he asked, "Lord, what about him?"

22 Jesus answered, "If I want him to remain alive until I return, what is that to you? You must follow me."

The moment their nets began to break because they were so filled with fish, Peter and John knew exactly what was happening. They had been fishing hundreds of times and this happened exactly once before.

Only Jesus. More than the wind and the waves—even the fish obey Him.

They got back to the beach, and once again, they were gathered around a fire. There are so many parallels in this story because Jesus was showing the disciples, and especially Peter, how it had all led to this moment.

A second miraculous catch of fish and a second conversation around a fire.

Jesus was not in a hurry. He took the time to enjoy the meal and to be with them. They all enjoyed the fish, but the miracle was bigger than fish—the real miracle was the restoration of Peter's relationship with Jesus.[6]

Jesus did not immediately get down to business. But once He did, He made it so simple with Peter.

"Do you love me . . . Feed my lambs."

Jesus did not ask Peter if he was sorry, if he had learned his lesson, or if he would mess up again. Jesus asked Peter if he still loved Him. That was the only lasting motivation that would sustain Peter.

And the way Peter showed he loved Jesus was by serving and leading the people. You may notice that Jesus asked Peter three times. One affirmation for each denial.

Peter may have given up on himself, but Jesus still had big plans for Peter. He wanted Peter to believe it too. Jesus

---

[6] The story is primarily about Peter but it also restored the other disciples to Jesus.

understood the restoration of Peter would lead to freedom and breakthrough for so many others.

He knew that in around 40 days, this same Peter would preach the first gospel message and thousands of people would repent and turn to Jesus.[7]

Jesus let Peter know this task was going to be difficult. He would be led where he did not want to go, but to remember that he was called to follow Jesus. Peter was processing all of this and basically asked Jesus, "What about John? What's going to happen to him?"

I love how the Bible reminds us these are real people who act like we do. And I appreciate the fact it's John who makes sure we know this about the story.

We don't all walk the same road. We don't all face the same challenges. This does not mean God loves some people more than others. Jesus tells Peter, "What's it to you?"

Jesus' love for Peter was not dependent upon what happened to John.

The same is true for us. When you are praying and trusting God to move, the temptation can be to see what your friends are going through. What did God do for them?

Stories of God's faithfulness are meant to encourage us because He is good. It's not meant to be a guarantee of what will, or won't, happen to us.

---
[7] Acts 2:14-41

Like Peter, you may feel like you've let Jesus down. At one point you felt so close. But now, because of some bad choices, you feel far from Him.

Or maybe you've looked at the things you've had to face and compared them to your friends. At times it has caused you to wonder if God had forgotten about you or if He was punishing you.

Miracles are a reminder of God's great love for us. He does not change. He is a loving Father who calls us home to Himself.

He sees you. He loves you. He has a Kingdom purpose for you as a member of His family. And like Peter, at times this road will be difficult. But Jesus makes it so simple.

Do you love Me? Follow Me.

REFLECTION QUESTIONS

Have you ever felt like you've disappointed God? If so, write down the last time you remember. Did it make you feel unworthy and distant from God?

After reading this chapter, what did you learn about Jesus?

Just like He did for Peter, Jesus can restore you. He can help you rediscover your purpose and calling.

Personalize this sample prayer and make it your own.

> *Jesus, I believe you come to restore us when we let you down. Please forgive me for* _____ [fill in your specific circumstance]. *You said in your Word that when*

we're faithful to confess our sin, you are faithful to cleanse us from all unrighteousness. Because of you, what happened in my past does not define my future. Help me to rediscover my purpose and calling in you. In Jesus' name I pray. Amen.

The Garden of Gethsemane

Conclusion

We have come to the end of this journey together, but my prayer for you is this would be a new beginning.

Whether you're still investigating this person Jesus or if you've known Him for a long time, I hope through these reflections on His miracles you have seen Him in a new light.

His person is even greater than His power. More than meeting our needs, His miracles reveal the depth of His love.

- He calmed the wind and the waves for His friends when they were afraid.
- He moved toward lepers everyone else feared.
- He called an unclean woman who had spent everything she had to try and cure a disease "daughter."
- He helped a worried father who believed his only daughter had died.
- He called a group of strangers friends because He was moved by their willingness

to help their paralyzed companion.
- He wept with two sisters experiencing the pain of loss before raising their brother from the dead.
- He restored one of His closest followers after his most public and humiliating failure.

This is Jesus.

There has never been anyone like Him. His miracle power established and accredited the power of God working through Him as the long-promised Son of God who would come to save the world.

And He delivered on the promise.

I don't know if you're praying for a miracle, but I know you have needs. When we have a need, we wonder, *Does God see what I'm going through? Does He care?*

My prayer is that, in reading these stories, you realize the overwhelming response from heaven is, "I see. I care. I am with you. I will never leave you or forsake you."

Though I can't definitively promise you the miracle you're praying for in the way and the timing you want it, I can boldly encourage you to keep asking. Jesus told us to ask, seek, and knock whenever we needed anything from the Father.[1]

---

[1] Matthew 7:7

You're probably thinking, *What if I ask and nothing happens? I don't know if I can handle the disappointment.* It's true. Getting our hopes up and praying big prayers make us vulnerable to discouragement.

But I've found whether or not we get discouraged, we're all still going to have needs. I would rather lean on the side of big prayers than keep quiet as a means to protect myself.

However, I can absolutely promise you the greatest and most important miracle of all time is available to all of us right now. The tomb is empty. Jesus did not stay dead.

He took on to Himself the weight of sin and death, all of your mistakes and my mistakes that separate us from the possibility of having a genuine relationship with a perfect God. His body was broken and His blood was poured out for the forgiveness of our sins. And on the third day after His death, He walked out of the tomb alive.

This is the greatest miracle of all because it allows anyone who would receive Him a new life in God. We can die to our sinful nature and be born again into a new and eternal life. The life we were created to live.

God didn't stop there. He also gave us His Word. What an incredible miracle He has given us to know the voice of God, to understand His nature and to grow in grace, wisdom, and knowledge as we spend time in the Bible.

We may take it for granted but for thousands of years (and still today in parts of the world) the typical follower of Christ had no access to a Bible. Guttenberg created the printing press in the 15th century in order for the whole world to be able to read God's Word.

There is nothing more valuable to help us grow closer to God and to know Him more than to regularly spend time reading the Bible.

Another important step for us to grow is to be connected to His family—the body of Christ—His Church. We are not meant to live the Christian life alone. If you don't already have a church family, I would love to help you find one.

His death and resurrection, His Word, and His Church are all supernatural expressions of the love of God and His desire to bring us into His family to help us grow. Maybe you never realized this, or maybe you needed a helpful reminder.

He wants us to know Him. To walk with Him. To experience His presence and peace in every area of our lives. He is better than we can imagine and He is still moving in miracle power.

Mountains in southern Isreal

APPENDIX

Small Group Study Guide

SMALL GROUP

Chapter 1
*What Happens in the
Storms of Life?*

Key Verse

"And he awoke and rebuked the wind and said to the sea, 'Peace! Be still!' And the wind ceased, and there was a great calm."

Mark 4:39, ESV

Discussion Questions

1. What things do people commonly fear?

2. What role does fear play in our culture? Is it big or small?

3. How do you typically respond to fear? Do you fight, run, or close your eyes and hope it goes away?

4. What is a better way to respond to fear?

5. Read Mark 4:37-38. What is Jesus doing while the disciples are afraid? What does this reveal?

6. In verse 38, the disciples ask Jesus a telling question: "Teacher, do you not care that we are perishing?" Have you ever faced a situation that made you wonder if God still cared about you? Explain.

7. When we face fearful situations, what is God trying to teach us?

Application Questions

What is the greatest challenge you're facing right now, and what is your greatest fear surrounding that challenge?

How does God want you to respond to the situation?

SMALL GROUP

Chapter 2
From the Outside In

Key Verse

"When he saw them, he said, 'Go, show yourselves to the priests.' And as they went, they were cleansed."

Luke 17:14

Discussion Questions

1. Read Luke 17:11-13. Why would it have been difficult for ten lepers even to approach Jesus?

2. What are some examples of modern-day "lepers" or outcasts in our culture? What should our response be to those who feel marginalized and mistreated?

3. Read Luke 17:14. How do you think the ten lepers felt when Jesus told them to show themselves to the priest before they were healed?

4. Why is obedience sometimes tied to a miracle?

5. Has God ever asked you to do something uncertain or risky? What was it, and what happened as a result?

6. Read Luke 17:15-16. Why does only one of the men come back to thank God? Why do you think the other nine did not return?

7. How quick are you to thank God when He blesses you?

Application Questions

What is something you are most grateful to God for right now?

What is something you will do this week to express your gratitude to God for His blessings?

SMALL GROUP

Chapter 3
Waiting on a Miracle

Key Verse

"Then he said to her, 'Daughter, your faith has
healed you. Go in peace.'"

Luke 8:48

Discussion Questions

1. Look at Luke 8:40-56. In what ways was Jairus's need
different from the woman's need? How were their needs
similar?

2. Have you ever needed an urgent miracle? What was it,
and what happened?

3. Have you ever waited on God for years to do a miracle? What was it, and what happened?

4. Read Luke 8:47-48. How did Jesus respond to the woman, and what did His response do for her?

5. Read Luke 8:49-50. What is Jesus trying to teach Jairus in this moment?

6. Why do you think we have to wait on God sometimes? What is God up to?

7. Think of a time you had to wait on God for something. What did God teach you during that season?

APPENDIX: SMALL GROUP STUDY GUIDE

Application Questions

Is there something you are currently waiting on God to do?
Is it something urgent, or have you been waiting a long
time? What is it?

How does God want you to respond while you wait?

SMALL GROUP

Chapter 4
Miracles with Friends

Key Verse

"When they could not find a way to do this because of the crowd, they went up on the roof and lowered him on his mat through the tiles into the middle of the crowd, right in front of Jesus. When Jesus saw their faith, he said, 'Friend, your sins are forgiven.'"

Luke 5:19-20

Discussion Questions

1. Read Luke 5:17-19. What do we learn about friendship from these verses?

2. Do you have friends like the men in this story—people who would do whatever it takes to help you out? Explain.

3. How can we find and cultivate deep friendships like this in our lives?

4. Tell us about a time you felt lonely. How did you make it through that time?

5. Read Luke 5:20. Why did Jesus say, "Friend, your sins are forgiven," instead of healing him physically right away?

6. What do we learn about Jesus from this story?

7. Is there someone you know who is struggling with a need? What can you do this week to be a friend to this person?

Application Questions

Are you currently struggling with loneliness? Explain

What's something you can do this week to combat the loneliness you feel?

SMALL GROUP

Chapter 5
*Finding Jesus in Our
Deepest Pain*

Key Verse

"Jesus said to her, 'I am the resurrection and the life. The one who believes in me will live, even though they die; and whoever lives by believing in me will never die. Do you believe this?'"

John 11:25-26

Discussion Questions

1. Read John 11:21 and 32. Why do you think Mary and Martha both said the same words to Jesus when they saw Him?

2. Have you ever felt like Mary and Martha in this story— "God, if you had shown up, this tragedy wouldn't have happened"? Tell us about it.

3. It's a natural human tendency to blame God when we experience pain and loss. Why is that?

4. Jesus waits long enough for Lazarus to die before He leaves Jerusalem. Why do you think Jesus waited?

5. Throughout the course of this book, we have seen multiple miracle stories where God waited before providing a miracle. What does this teach you about God?

6. Read John 11:33-35. Why does Jesus weep? What does this reveal about God?

7. How do you think Mary, Martha, and Lazarus saw Jesus differently as a result of this miracle?

Application Questions

Are you facing a painful situation in life right now? What is it?

What do you think God is trying to teach you in the season you're in?

SMALL GROUP

Chapter 6
The Second Fire

Key Verse

"When they had finished eating, Jesus said to Simon Peter, 'Simon son of John, do you love me more than these?' 'Yes, Lord,' he said, 'you know that I love you.' Jesus said, 'Feed my lambs.'"

John 21:15

Discussion Questions

1. Going through this study, what have you learned about the primary reason God performs miracles?

2. Read John 21:1-3. Why did Peter go back to fishing?

3. Have you ever felt like you failed God? How did you respond to the failure?

4. Read John 21:4-6. Why does Jesus perform the same miracle here as when He first called Peter? (See Luke 5:1-11 for the original miracle.)

5. Read John 21:15-17. Jesus asks Peter three times, "Do you love Me?" What does this reveal about God when we fail?

6. What is Jesus ultimately up to in this miracle story?

7. Have you experienced a time when God restored you? Tell us about it.

Application Questions

Are you struggling in your relationship with God for any reason? If so, how can we pray for you?

What do you feel like God would say to you right now?

ALSO FROM JEFF LITTLE

VISIT US ONLINE!

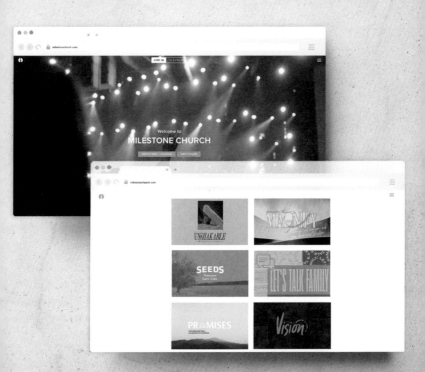

MILESTONECHURCH.COM

CONNECT WITH JEFF LITTLE

📷 @JEFFLITTLE

🐦 @JEFF_LITTLE

f @PASTORJEFFLITTLE